BEYOND
the Skies of Blue and Pink

K. L. NELSON

ISBN 979-8-89043-794-5 (paperback)
ISBN 979-8-89043-796-9 (hardcover)
ISBN 979-8-89043-795-2 (digital)

Christian Faith Publishing
832 Park Avenue
Meadville, PA 16335
www.christianfaithpublishing.com

Printed in the United States of America

Chapter 1

On November 8, 2020, my husband of twenty-six years died, and a part of me died with him.

I know I am not the only one to ever experience grief, and all of us handle our pain and heartache differently. I don't personally believe anyone knows how they will handle a loss when that time comes. Every loss is significant, but the loss of my husband was not only significant but had been completely life-changing and had a glaring impact on my life.

No one truly knows or understands what someone is going through after losing the love of their life and how alone you feel after losing the one person you have ever loved since you were fifteen.

There is nothing fun, normal, or easy about learning to live life on your own for the first time at forty-seven years old, trying to figure out who you are as an individual in what now seems like a very empty and completely different world.

The first moments after learning of my husband's passing, I was numb, and I felt empty inside; my entire being felt shallow and void of itself. I had reverted inward to a world of shock and confusion. It was as if I were in the middle of a nightmare that I couldn't scream my way out of, walking through empty hallways dismissive of any sounds around me.

I was completely lost in my own thoughts, and I felt like I was in hell.

I had involuntary moments, where the silence around me would break with an eruption of sobbing tears that led to me hyperventilating, at which point, one of my four boys would wrap their arms around me, trying to comfort me. Each of them would take turns, and they told me that they would see my hands start to shake as I was staring off into an empty space, and that was enough to know that one of them would need to brace the dam that was ready to break once again.

I had no appetite and no interest in even trying to eat as much as my boys tried to insist that I needed to.

The ability to fall asleep was impossible. At one point, my son Brendan sat beside me and gently rubbed my back. For the first time in seventy-two hours, I slept for thirty minutes, only to wake up in tears at the realization that the nightmare I was in the middle of was, in fact, a reality.

Waking up alone and laying down in an empty bed at night have been the hardest parts of every day since that wretched moment in time. The habitual daily behaviors are vastly different now, and I am still struggling with the changes.

I struggle every day to feel the normalcy of life that I once had—or at least what I believed was a normal life. Prior to my husband's passing, I started an online blog called "KristaBell's Ponders," where I had been freelance writing personal opinion blogs. A short time after losing him, I started writing these blogs with regard to the emotions and the thoughts I was enduring in hopes to get myself through the pain, heartache, and emptiness that I consistently felt. It really did make a difference to write it all out, and it had carried me through some of the most difficult moments and continues to.

It has been almost two years, and I am still having nightmares about the last evening I spent with my husband and the morning of his death. Sometimes, the nightmares have no correlation; they are just strange, eerie, creepy dreams.

I won't lie, but sometimes, I dream of some of the bad moments I had with my husband in the past. I have mornings when I wake up angry at the world because I have to start over, angry that I have to adjust to a change I never asked for, and angry because I do not understand why my path in life came with such dips and turns.

There even have been fits of anger toward him and the fact that I now have to live in this world alone and handle all the responsibilities of our life on my own.

There are songs, movies, surroundings, and moments each day that make me think of him, and there are times when those thoughts turn into uncontrollable outbursts of tears, accompanied by the inability to catch my breath.

I can only hope that at some point, the memories of that treacherous day will become less painful and less prominent in my mind. I continue to pray that, God willing, the good memories and the happy times will overpower the heartache of losing him, but of course, it is those memories that make me miss him the most.

Through my faith, I know that I will see him again someday, and that keeps the pain at bay.

My heart breaks for my children and the loss they, too, will feel for the rest of their lives. I always believe myself to be a strong woman and a good mom, but at this moment, I feel weak and as if I haven't been strong enough for them. I feel as if I lost myself in my own pain, focusing only on my own feelings, and now I realize, I must remember theirs, too, and be the strength they need me to be.

I miss our family, my children being little, and the idea of my husband and I spending the rest of our lives together. The conversation of someday being grandparents—the laughter when we spoke of someday having the house to ourselves again and enjoying our grandbabies, just knowing we could send them home at the end of the day and relish in the comfort of knowing we did well and we held on to each other through it all. We always believed that we were the greatest couple; however, I am sure every couple believes that.

Now, I see that we were a strong couple with weaknesses as individuals. We needed each other for support through our own issues that we carried in life—our own individual heartaches and struggles. We weren't a perfect couple, but we were definitely a dynamic one.

I believe that the Lord placed the two of us in each other's paths all those years ago because he knew, as a young man and woman, that we would need each other. He knew that life was going to test us both at a young age. I was the warm touch and the grounding he needed while he was the strength I needed. We both gave each other comfort; he helped me find confidence in myself, and I gave him a shining light to come home to and a loving comfort to hold onto until that one fateful moment when he headed toward the Lord's light instead of mine.

I believe it was then that God decided that my husband's journey was complete, and now, after replaying previous conversations with my husband, I believe he also knew this to be true.

I spent thirty-two years loving the man of my dreams and fighting with him and alongside him to achieve the life that we both dreamed of. I had spent the last twenty-seven years feeling like the most blessed mama in the world, with the greatest boys anyone could ever have. I loved being a wife, and I love being a mother. Even with all the roughest moments along the way, I know I have had a blessed life.

My greatest desire as a wife and a mother was to be the very best—to make sure that my husband and my children were always placed first and given the best care and all of my love. I was determined to be their strength and mine. I believed, and still do, that was how a good wife and mother was measured.

I also believe that what defines a good teammate, partner, spouse, and friend is someone who will stand the test of time with you, through thick and thin, good times and bad. Someone who will love you through it all, forever and always. I know the two of us had that.

What I didn't realize was how great a toll all those years had on me, and what I am realizing now is that I have never taken any time to find out who I am and what I want out of this life. I believed I already had everything I could ever want and more. I have come to understand now that I haven't even begun to scratch the surface on the life I was meant to live.

I am now beginning to process fully how much of my life was about him and how little it was about me. I know he loved me, and I know he would have given his life for me, but somewhere along the way, I was so busy finding my happiness in making him happy that I never stopped to think about having a true happiness of my own. I felt as if seeing my husband and my children smile and be happy was all the happiness I needed in life.

Don't get me wrong; it certainly had been rewarding and had made my life feel full. It just wasn't the full and complete purpose of my life, and I think it is fair to say it certainly wasn't the entirety of my dreams.

It was an incredible beginning, a tough challenge, and one hell of a start to my life.

You must have challenges in life in order to be able to endure all the obstacles life will throw your way. It's how we learn to find our strength.

We must first learn to fight and, with that, learn how to go on. We will never learn how to succeed if we never enter the battle. Fulfilling all your hopes and dreams is a great endeavor; fulfilling your whole life's purpose is done only through the will of God. I aspire to achieve both.

I have found that God has already given me everything I could ever need in life, and it surrounds me every day. The rest of my life is mine for the taking.

I do not need millions of dollars or material objects, but instead, I choose to receive all my happiness from the beauty that surrounds me—to absorb all of nature's treasures, to find my smile through my children, my love, the stars, the flowers, the blue waters, the soft sands, and through having the faith to place my entire life in God's hands.

My life remains guided by faith, daisies, and sky blue pink. Every direction in my life is pointed out by these three things, and it has always served me well.

My life has been far from perfect, but it has certainly taught me how perfect life truly is if you just believe it to be. That is the story I wish to share with you today. I am no longer looking for the perfect life or seeking perfection in myself. I am only looking for a life that is perfect for me and a me that is perfect for the ones I love.

I have always believed that a woman carries herself with dignity, grace, class, and style. A woman holds her faith in the Lord and her pride in the good deeds she has done, measured only by the Lord. I believe a woman acts with decorum and has strengths a man could never hold.

I believe in marriage and the entirety of its vows, and I believe in the gift of life and life beginning at conception. I believe in being responsible for your own actions and being strong enough to be the blessing that loves someone through some of their worst actions.

Since the day I lost my husband, I have been searching for who I am without him. I know who I was with him. I was a loving and doting wife, a blessed and happy mother of four beautiful boys, and a woman who believed I had everything I could have ever hoped for—a life completely blessed and utterly full.

These last two years have been a continuous ride for me and, quite frankly, a journey I never saw coming.

Chapter 2

After my husband passed away, there was an incredible change in me. I no longer felt like the same human being I once was. My love and desire for nursing was just not there anymore. My thoughts about life in general had changed significantly, and the life I was living suddenly took a one-hundred-and-eighty-degree turn from every plan I had in place for my life.

I suddenly had an entirely new way of thinking. I now have a brand new plan for the kind of life I want to live from now on. The life I had with my husband is in my past now, and I am on a new and boundless journey to fulfill all my happiness and all my dreams, and I will never settle for anything less for the rest of my life.

It's funny how nothing feels the same after you experience such an immense loss in your life. The world looks completely different, and you suddenly see everything in your life in a very interesting new light.

Recently, it has become clear to me that I do not need a wealth of money to make me happy. I need to live my life, I need to enjoy my last child growing up, and I need to be happy and free from anyone and anything that makes me feel discouraged, angry, and fed up. My true happiness is in everything I already have and anything I desire to achieve. Through all of my husband's fighting for what he wanted out of life, I believe this truth is what he failed to understand the most. I think if he had, he would not have let what he lacked get the best of him and create the stress that took his life way too soon.

In this new rebirth of life for me, I have come to understand what he could not. I have been given the chance to see what we were both missing. I need to stop living for the material things and just start living—period. I need to go on with my life and live for myself and my children now. I need to love again and feel loved again. I am learning now that it is possible to love again, and I am capable of loving again. This time around, it will not just be a love at first sight, but a chance to measure someone's worth for my love.

To my surprise, I recently found myself being given this chance. I fought it at first and denied my feelings, and I believe the Lord fought me back. It seemed no matter how hard I tried to deny my affection for this man, I kept returning to him and wanting to spend more time around him. I needed this man to check every box I had for being the right fit for me. I needed to be extremely confident when it came to giving my heart to someone again.

Unbeknownst to me, I was not the only one questioning this new relationship. A young lady came to me and addressed me on my actions toward this man. She questioned why I was taking the time to confirm if what we had between us was strong enough to be real love. She gave me the impression that she believed that my intentions were ingenuine and could quite possibly lead to the hurt and heartache of a person she and I both love. I know one day, this young lady will think better of me, and I know she will undoubtedly realize the genuineness of my love and affection soon enough. She is a sweet soul, and of course, she is. She was raised well and by a terrific man with the sweetest of souls himself.

The truth is, I was guarding us both from any unnecessary hurt or heartache. I could never hurt this person or anyone that I care about, and I was not willing to allow myself, my family, or his to be hurt by quick reactions and irresponsible decisions.

For me, giving my heart to someone is a commitment. I do not play with people's hearts, and I do not take the word "love" lightly. I could never be the single girl who dates around. The one thing I have learned about myself is that I love having a partner, a best friend, a companion, and a lover. Not someone for the moment, but someone for every moment.

I loved my husband with all my heart and soul. I cherished our marriage, and I took seriously our vows to each other. I do not believe in divorce as an easy answer. I believe communication is key and necessary to every relationship's success, and when you give yourself to someone, it's because you know, with no uncertainty, that they are the perfect one for you and there will be no other.

The Bible holds the only reference to what is expected of you when it comes to consummating a relationship between one another. Those are sacred words and vital to who I am. Of course, I am not perfect, and I am not without fault of my own. I am not flawless with regard to the Lord's scripture and expectation.

I am human and sometimes naive to someone's play on truth and honesty, but I am strong on my beliefs and how I carry myself as a dignified and true lady. Nothing matters to me more than my own self-respect and being respectful to others.

Self-respect is a tough challenge that I think you fight to take ownership of all your life.

I have always been okay with not being the most important person in the room. I have always been just fine not being the center of attention. I have pretty much been a very quiet, reserved person and a bit shy until my husband's passing. It was then I realized that he was always my light in the room; he was the person everyone noticed first, and I was great with that until now. Now, if I want to be noticed, I have to speak up, I have to shine, and I have to find a way to make my presence known all on my own. For me, self-confidence is my greatest challenge.

I let everyone in my life take center stage because I love to watch them shine, and truthfully, I am not a fan of the spotlight. I stand in the back, being the caregiver, the nurturer, and the cheerleader because it is where I feel I fit best. You learn pretty quickly when you willingly work behind the scenes that you get taken advantage of quite a bit.

It's not the ideal role for everyone, but for some of us, we seem to not even notice until one day, it smacks us right in the face.

That day came for me nineteen months after I lost my husband. It was a difficult feeling to endure, and it still is. Realizing years later that everything you went through had an intense impact on you, that still makes you react negatively and nervously to certain behaviors. My mind still has not lost the fear of someone sneaking away, and I am still fighting the anguish of someone sneaking behind my back to achieve their own personal bad habits. More than that, I am terrified of falling in love again and losing that person to those horrible habits.

Today, I believe the Lord has placed me in a new path alongside a wonderful man, and once again, I believe there is purpose. I believe we have found one another along our own diverted paths in order to give comfort to one another and to be the light for each other as we challenge ourselves to live the life we both deserve. I believe in soulmates, and I know the Lord has blessed me with finding mine for the second time.

It was Christmas Eve thirty years ago when I first met my second soulmate. I, of course, did not see him as this back then, but I knew from that first interaction that he was someone I would never forget.

My boyfriend and I were attending his work Christmas party. I was a young girl of eighteen. I was nervous and shy, and I stayed put in the back of the room. My boyfriend was always the life of the party or at least a big part of it. He was off mingling as I stood alone, people-watching and wishing I was home. It was then I took notice of this young man noticing me. It was not long before he was heading my way. As he approached me, he reached out for my hand and introduced himself as a member of the family who owned the company my boyfriend was working for. Shy as I was, I engaged him, shook his hand, and introduced myself to him in return.

Without another wasted second, he asked me to come with him—to where I had no idea. At that very moment, my boyfriend made his way over to where we were and made it known that I was with him. The young man responded as he continued to hold my hand, gazing upon the bareness of it, "I do not see a ring on this hand." My boyfriend's response was nothing kind.

From that day forward, every year, at every company event, that man would address me with a hug. One, to my surprise, I looked forward to every year.

It was always this young man's lighthearted gest toward my husband that should he ever let me go, he would be there to pursue me.

There was always laughter to follow. Of course, none of us believed that moment would ever transpire.

To our surprise, this moment actually became a reality. A reality that has found us feeling as if we had always had a destiny in life with each other, but we just couldn't have ever known when.

Oddly enough, thirty years after our first meeting, my life spun out of control, and at the same time, so did his. While I was in shock over the unexpected loss of my husband, he was enduring his own loss, closing the chapter on an unhappy relationship.

Upon arriving home from the hospital, where I had confirmed the death of my dear husband, I knew I needed to make a few calls—at least I felt I needed to. My husband's phone had been unavailable to me at the time, and the numbers I would need to reach friends and family were all in it, except one.

The young man of thirty years ago, his name and number were written on a sticky note, smack-dab in the middle of my husband's desk. Outside of my immediate family and my husband's, he was the first person I called.

Neither one of us had any thought in mind that this would be our first connection to the rest of our lives together.

Chapter 3

I can say, without any uncertainty today, neither one of us had any plans to fall in love again. While I was feeling as if my entire heart and soul had been ripped from my being, he was entirely fed up with never finding the one that would make his heart and soul feel completely full. We had no idea we were the answer for each other—the answer we were both searching for and that together we would heal one another.

Almost a year and a half after my husband's passing, I made plans to take a trip to my hometown to visit family and friends. I made mention of this plan on social media, and once again, he took notice. He reached out to ask if I could make time for him and join him for dinner. I must admit I was happily surprised and kindly accepted the invite. It was then that I became nervous. I told myself it was just a dinner between friends until amidst my asking if he would be bringing his love. I learned they were no longer together, and he would be coming alone.

This would be the first time we would be in each other's company without anyone to prevent any feelings from becoming a reality. I honestly had no idea how I would feel about him or what he would or would not be feeling toward me. What I knew for certain was that everything in my life at this point was in God's hands, and I was giving him full control of the wheel.

A few weeks later, it was time to make the trip. What I haven't shared with you is that I had canceled the dinner with him after his excitement got the best of him and scared me off just a bit. After a great deal of thinking things over with regard to my quick reaction to cancel, I reinitiated the dinner plans, and he graciously accepted. The Lord was certainly playing his hand in this, and I knew it.

I made my way home to see my family and friends—a much needed trip for myself and my loved ones. The night had come to meet for dinner, and I was a nervous wreck. I changed outfits three times, and the butterflies in my stomach were on full throttle.

I must admit I already had some idea of what to expect. I had met with him a few nights before after some previous plans had canceled, and I was looking for something else to do.

I called him to see if we could get together to break the ice. He willingly agreed and invited me to his place. We spent the evening catching up and getting reacquainted. It had been a few years since we had last seen each other. A lot of things were brought to light about one another, and it became a very relaxed evening of drinks and great conversation. We learned fairly quickly that there was definite chemistry between the two of us, and I learned he had definite feelings for me. However, I was still trying to realize my feelings for him.

We met a few days later for our dinner date at a beautiful restaurant. He was quite the gentleman and made me feel like a princess the entire evening. Everything between us was so relaxed and so easy, it actually scared me. I worried that the feelings I was having were happening too quickly, and I was concerned I would end up hurt. I had no room for that. I was also not willing to hurt him by jumping into things too soon and without any vetting process between us. I agreed to a second date before the week's end, and I also accepted another invite for a date with someone else—a dear friend, who will always be my dear friend, but not meant to be a love interest for me. Not a decision I had come to right away.

The week had come to an end, and now, I was headed home, six hundred miles away to think things through. I waited out the time to see if either date would call, and much to my surprise, I only continued to hear from one of them—the one I somehow knew all along, felt completely right, and yet, I fought my own self in believing it to be true.

Every response he gave to every question I had or story I shared was the right one. We had so many things in common and shared the same values, impeccably, to a tee. It quite honestly scared the hell out of me, and at the same time, I found myself falling for him even more. I just had to be sure. I had to make sure, without any hesitation, that this was right. I couldn't allow either of us to be hurt or either of our families to be dragged through any more grief.

Months later, during a visit to see him, I was certain he had checked all the boxes, and I told him so. He is an incredible man with a heart of gold. The Lord has truly blessed me with a soulmate for the second time.

Our children are not so easily convinced that our choices are sound and that we have found exactly who we belong with at this time in our lives. We both know, in time, they will understand and believe in our love for each other. Someday, they will all find comfort in knowing that we were meant for one another at this time in our lives, and what we have is solid and strong.

I cannot and I will not tell you that falling in love again has stopped me from loving and missing my dear husband because it has not. That is a love and a heartache that I know, with every certainty in my life, will never end.

What I can tell you is the Lord created a life journey for me that was never meant to be without love, and I will forever be grateful and will always know how blessed I truly am.

Our lives do not come with an instruction manual or a list of time frames that lay out when changes will occur within them. We are not guided by outlines or deadlines but instead, by faith, love, and hope. As human beings, we are inspired, encouraged, determined, and insistent when searching for what we want for ourselves and the life we desire to live.

As the Lord's chosen souls, we are souls that have been given the blessing to live on this earth, prove our worth, and find our faith in him. We were created with hearts that are meant to guide and enable us to feel the rights and wrongs for each of us individually. Our hearts are not the most perfect organ; they do also enable us to feel pain and heartache, but I believe the Lord intended such feelings to give us the ability to understand his pain and to reach for his guidance through our faith in him.

If we had not been given a heart, we could not feel the pounding and pulsating beat of it when we are falling in love or the intense and rapid sensation of it when we feel true excitement and joy. We would be without the ability to care, and without that, what kind of world would we live in then?

We cannot presume to know when the timing is right to feel love or even if we will ever feel love again, especially after a tragic, heart-wrenching loss of someone we never imagined we would be living without. Our hearts do not hold clocks, watches, or any other measures of time; they provide us the ability to feel. They allow us the opportunity to give of ourselves and to receive unto ourselves when it feels right to do so. Only God can judge whether our feelings and the choices we make, based on them, are right or wrong.

I never felt I would love again, but the good Lord knew otherwise. His plan for me was much different than mine, and he let me know.

As I said before, I know now I am capable of loving again, and I deserve to love again. I have found someone that has made it easy to want to love again. I can only hope—and I do believe—I have done the same for him.

My greatest desire in this world is for my children to someday know that same feeling of love because it is the most incredible feeling they will ever receive. I loved their dad with all my heart and every fiber of my being, and I know he loved me just the same. My tears will never completely dry up and go away, but perhaps someday, they will only be tears of joy for what I had and not tears of anguish for what left me that one fateful day.

I have found happiness again, my smile has returned, and my heart has filled a new place in it. I am so grateful for you, my love. Thank you, Lord, for blessing me so graciously once again.

In a world full of love and hate, happiness and heartache, prosperity and poverty, and life and death, we can only hope to find ourselves enjoying all the positive parts of each equation.

The very nature of the world we live in requires each one of us to battle through the negative pieces to get to the positive. A fight that is meant to provide us the opportunity to prove our faith and find strength in ourselves and the Lord. We do all this so that we might live a life filled with peace and tranquility. We do all of this so that when our time comes to pass on, we know that we gave it our all and we lived our best life during our time here on earth.

How do we get there? We place our lives in God's hands; we trust in him and have faith that if we live by his plan, he will never let us fall. I have been in the training stages of this way of living for quite a while, but only since the loss of my husband have I taken the full reins and handed them over to him. I cannot wait to tell you how it has changed my life and the happiness it has given me.

Chapter 4

I spent my entire life believing in God, and I spent my entire childhood telling myself I would follow every commandment he gave, but I faltered. I have sinned and come short of the glory of God, but I have never stopped believing and I have always kept my faith in the Lord.

I have asked for his forgiveness more than once, and I have placed my life in his hands many times. I have asked for him to carry me through the greatest storms of my life throughout the years, and he has carried me through every single one.

I am not sure anything in this lifetime prepares you for the death of someone you love, but I do believe that the Lord does his best to make you aware of its coming, and he certainly gave us a few signs, as you may have read in my previous book.

As I mentioned before, at the bedside of my deceased husband, I was not a frantic woman and I was not screaming, but instead, I was sobbing and speaking to him as if I believed he could hear me. I held his hand, still warm to the touch, and I let him know I was there. I tried desperately to find understanding of why this was happening. I had two of my boys standing beside me, crying, and visibly shaken. Together, we prayed for guidance and for the Lord to see our dear husband and father home to paradise peacefully. I left his side and the hospital in shock, and I remained that way for the next few days.

On the fourth day after my husband's passing, I gave everything I had to the Lord. I sat at the side of my bed, and I told the Lord I had nothing left in me. I let him know that I was at a loss for what to do next, and I asked him to take the wheel.

And he did.

From that day forward, I have continued to talk to him and my dearly departed husband every day. I have shared every thought I have with them, good and bad. I have asked them to guide me through every concern I have and every decision and action I make.

And they do.

I would be remiss if I do not include the continued guidance of my grandmothers and the skies of blue and pink that continue to arise every time I am searching for an answer or the daisies that have appeared when I need confirmation on a decision I have made. If I have learned anything from the moments up to my husband's passing, I have learned the difference in the meaning of the messages my grandmothers are providing by the shade of pink that presents in the sky.

The darkest shade is my warning, whatever it may be, and the light, translucent shade is letting me know that I am doing fine, that my actions are good, and my decisions are right.

It was after a beautiful bouquet of sky blue and pink roses with white and blue daisies arrived at my door that I knew the man who sent them was a decision I made well and the right choice for me.

Almost a year after that tragic day of November 2020, it was midsummer, and I was sitting on my front porch, talking to the Lord. While discussing with the Lord my thoughts on what I needed to focus on now in my life, a light breeze began to tussle my hair as I felt the warmth of the sun on my face. A flock of red robins landed in my yard, not two or three, but ten or more. I watched them bounce around the yard, and I listened to their song as they looked about. There was one that stood dead center in my yard and looked straight at me for just a moment, longer than a second but less than a full minute.

It was as if the spirit of my husband was within that beautiful little bird and was saying, "I am always here, my love. You are never alone." I could smell the sweetness in the air and feel a sudden peace all around me. I was filled with a warmth throughout my entire body.

It was at that very moment I realized the Lord was telling me, "This is your focus, your only focus. I have given you everything you need. Look around you, stop suffering and fighting, and enjoy what you already have. Life is too short to miss all of the beauty in it by working so hard and being so miserable doing so. I will give you what you need if you just believe in me. Have faith in the decisions I make for you, and you will see just how happy you can be."

On that day, at that moment, I lost all of my anger, my frustration, and my fear, and I started over for me, for my children, and for the Lord.

Every one of us has spent our lives busting our butts to get where we are. Are you where you want to be? Are you happy? Are you at peace with the life you have built and the life you are leading? Do you get up every morning excited for the job you are headed to? Does your job give you everything you desire in your life?

I am guessing for most of you, the answer to these questions is a resounding no. Do you understand why? I don't have all the answers because I don't know all your lives and how you are living them, but I have a theory. My theory is this: we are not where we want to be, and we are not the happy we desire to be. We all have parts of our life that we are not at peace with, and most of us do not get up in the morning happy with where we are headed, and it's doubtful that your job is giving you everything you desire in life. Why? The answer is simple. We have neglected to take the time to stop and see all the beauty and gifts God has already given to us.

We are missing the point that life is not about what we desire, but what we already have. If we do not stop now and enjoy what we have, we will have missed it all, and it will be too late to get it back. Life is short, it goes by in an instant, and sometimes, it ends way to soon. We can never know when our time will come, but what we do know is that we have time now to stop and enjoy what surrounds us every day. Find happiness and joy in what you already have, and find the beauty in what already exists. Do whatever it is that brings you the greatest happiness because that is worth more than any dollar you might earn and any object you might own.

You cannot bring the material things with you, but you can bring with you the peace and joy of knowing that you lived the best life you could have and that, one day, your faith in the Lord will bring you home to paradise.

You may think everything I just said is foolish and ridiculous. You might very well be sitting here thinking it's not worth the risk. You are probably thinking, *I have to work this miserable job to pay the bills and take care of my family.* What you don't see is that you really don't. Yes, you need to pay your bills and support your family, but you do not have to settle for a job that takes away your joy in life.

Anyone of us can do whatever we desire in life if we just make the effort and if we just stop searching for more and start living for what we already have.

God gave us everything in this world that we need to survive; we are the greedy ones looking for more.

God gave me one of the best guides in my life, one that I have not shared with you. She is one of the most important—my mother. During my childhood, my mother endured many tested moments and many life-altering situations. As I watched her go through some of these moments, I learned what not to do and how to handle things a bit differently than she did. I also learned what not to allow to ever happen in my life. My mother took steps in her life that I never wish to follow, and I am forever grateful that she took those steps because, whether she knows it or not, she took those steps for me.

What I have learned is that my mother took those steps and made those choices in hopes that I would never have to and afforded me the opportunity to learn to do better or change direction. This does not mean that my mom made poor choices but rather that she took the first steps to make sure I didn't hit any land mines along my path in life. She will never understand how thankful I am to her for taking those first steps in front of me to shield me and guide me in making different choices toward my destinations in life. She will always be the wind beneath my wings.

Every one of us has someone that has inspired us, someone or something that guides us, and for some of us, we have a higher power that keeps us grounded, gives us purpose, and leads our plan for the path we follow in our lives. If you don't, if you are not sure you do, or if you believe you haven't found it, do yourself a favor and start looking for it. Open your hearts and your minds, and think about what or who led you to where you are today. Do they carry enough positive weight in your life to continue to be your someone or something that inspires you, guides you, and shows you a path to keep following that finds you every happiness you can imagine for the rest of your life?

I know for me, there are many who have been an inspiration in my life. As a child, my life began with the inspiration of my parents and my grandmothers from a very young age. It was then and as a young student that I learned about God, and I accepted him as my savior and the leader of my path in life.

During my time in school, it was a fifth-grade teacher, who inspired me to not just read the Word of God, but to hear it and feel it. She introduced me to the music of Amy Grant, and her music helped me to feel my love for God and realize how he impacts my life every day. I will forever be thankful for that teacher, and I can never begin to tell her what she means to me.

As a teenager, it was my first boyfriend, who later became my husband, that inspired me to have confidence and strength in myself. He was my first feeling of unconditional love, and together, previous to our marriage, we were both baptized through the eyes of the Lord. As a young married woman, our children inspired me to be a good mom, holding a love for them that is beyond measure and has no barriers. Watching my boys grow into the men they are today and seeing all they have achieved give me the satisfaction of knowing that my husband and I did our job well. My boys give me a reason to carry on and to reach every goal I aspire to achieve so that they might see that they can too. My greatest hope is to be one of their inspirations in life as well.

As a widowed woman today, it is my new love that inspires me. He inspires me to challenge myself, to reach for everything I desire, and to achieve it. He has given me the ability to realize that I can love and feel that unconditional love once again. He makes me feel beautiful inside and out. He walks beside me, not behind me or in front of me. He inspires me to want to be the best teammate, partner, friend, and lover I can be, and he makes it easy for me to do so.

I have said it before that life was never supposed to be easy. It is God's test to see what we are made of and whether we will find our faith in him and allow him to lead us. Our challenge is to be humble enough to know we can't live this life on our own and to understand that we can make it through every struggle and every hurdle, and find every triumph with greater ease if we just find within ourselves that we believe.

I know my husband believed in God, I just wish he had faith enough to let God lead his life so that he might have been able to let go of the burdens he carried and the worries he held. Maybe then he would have found that greater ease with life and the hurdles we always seemed to be climbing. Perhaps if he could have given it all to God, his heart would have taken much less of a beating, and he would still be alive today.

I didn't see the warnings that came before he passed, but he did, and maybe it was then that he finally let God take the wheel and understood that God would be leading him home. If there was anywhere other than here that I would wish him to be, it is in paradise, finding all the peace he so greatly deserves. My love for him will always be eternal, and I hope that I am making him proud as my life continues to go on.

Chapter 5

In early January of 2022, I was having one of my morning conversations with the Lord while enjoying my coffee. Conversations where I talk, and he listens, and I know he is listening. I was praying to get the job that I had recently interviewed for and asking the Lord to let the ladies I interviewed with see my worth and to find in their hearts that I was the person they were looking for. I shared with the Lord that morning that I had a list of goals I was still hoping to achieve, and I knew I would need to do some work to get there, and I would need him to see me through.

I discussed with the Lord all the dreams I hoped to achieve. Dreams to have a house on the lake where I could live out the rest of my life—a dream my husband I both shared. Dreams to find a job that gave me a sense of reward for the work I was doing and to hopefully not have to spend the rest of my life alone, even though I wondered if I would be capable of loving again. In gest, I also mentioned a Chevy Camaro convertible that I would love to have someday.

I spoke to the spirit of my husband that morning as well and told him I would always do my best to make him proud, that I loved him and that should I ever find love again, my love for him would always be the same. I asked him to help me to know when that love had found me. I told him to continue to watch over our babies and to find a way to always let them know he was with them.

It was just a few days later when I got the call letting me know they had chosen me for the job. A couple of weeks beyond that, I received a text message inviting me to dinner from the man that would be the love that would come along, and it was a few months into conversations with him that I learned he in fact owned a house on the lake. This, of course, had no bearing on whether he was the right one for me, but it certainly was an uncanny coincidence, to say the least.

After eight months of conversation, four months of dating, and a few strenuous lists of positives and negatives with regard to our thoughts and plans of a possible future together, I am now living on that lake, in that very house, with that incredible man that I could not help but fall in love with.

As I said before, nothing comes with a time frame attached, but I do believe every great thing comes through faith.

Sitting here today on the wraparound deck of my home—a deck that overlooks the beautiful blue waters of one of the greatest freshwater lakes in the world and one of the best sugar sand beaches; a deck that is connected to a home I share with the most wonderful man, who continues to make me wonder what I did to deserve his love—I know that the Lord is not only listening to me, but that he has blessed me with every hope and dream I spoke of earlier this year. While lying on the beach just yesterday, I came to the sudden realization that yesterday, today, tomorrow, and every day after, I have everything I have ever wanted and I have achieved everything I have ever desired up until this point, but I am not done yet.

I want to keep writing, and I am hopeful that my writing will inspire others. I am hopeful to one day be a grandmother and perhaps even a great-grandmother, and my greatest dream is to one day see my boys achieve all their dreams.

It makes me wonder if some of these dreams would have ever become a reality should my dearly departed husband still had been alive. I know for certain my first book would never have been written not because I was not inspired to write back then, but because he was not one to share personal things with others and would never have been okay with the idea. I believe our story is special and worth sharing, and I hope he is up there seeing that today.

I know I would never have acquired the rewarding job I did because it would not have lent enough hours of work in his belief and the pay would not have been enough. He wanted me to be the primary breadwinner in order to afford him the opportunity, at some point, to change direction and achieve his dream of owning a brewery.

Could it be that each one of us not only have a planned path to walk in life, but that we all have a direction through God to achieve, and once the work he has meant for us to do is complete, it is then that our time on earth is done? Are we all souls of God that are meant to be beacons that fulfill a purpose and carry out a task, one that God has chosen for us?

Is it possible that we might come to a point in life where we no longer have a destiny to reach or a reason to continue and that is when our life here on earth comes to an end? Only God knows these answers.

I think it is possible for the Lord to look upon each one of us and see those who have lost their hope and exhausted their willingness to continue on. I believe he sees those enduring a pain they can no longer take and those who have no strength left to fight, and it is then that he takes them home. The Lord answers this best in the King James version of the Bible in Matthew 19:14: *"Jesus said, suffer little children, and forbid them not, to come unto me: for of such is the kingdom of heaven."*

For me, two of the greatest verses and words my grandmothers held dear to their hearts are John 3:16, which says, *"For God so loved the world that he gave his only begotten son, that whosoever believeth in him, shall not perish but have everlasting life;"* and John 14:1–3, which says, *"Let not your heart be troubled: ye believe in God, believe also in me. In my Father's house are many mansions: if it were not so, I would have told you. I go to prepare a place for you and if I go and prepare a place for you, I will come again, and receive you unto myself; that where I am, there ye may be also."*

With a word such as this, I cannot help but believe and know in my heart that all of us have a planned path laid out and destined by God. It is up to each one of us how we follow that plan, whether we let God lead or we take the reins ourselves, and hope we reach the destiny he has chosen. We all must suffer in order to become humble in this life and find the acceptance that we cannot live this life without faith in God, and we will never achieve our dreams and find eternal bliss without him in our hearts.

I do not believe that God wants any of us to suffer, but that we as humans never seem to see the light until we have reached the darkness. I do not believe God sends the plagues of disease to us. Those are brought from evil, from the pits of hell, and the devil himself. Those are created by the works of human hands.

The good Lord is the one who stops our pain because he believes we have suffered enough. He does not wish to watch the delicate soul he placed on this earth go through anymore. When he feels our faith in him, it is then that he wraps his arms around our fragile souls and carry us home.

My husband used to say that he lived a great life, and that he had lived a full life. He would say, "I have done it all and had a blast doing it. If I left this earth today, I know I have taught my sons well, I know they will take care of you, and that I have impressed upon them what knowledge I had to share in order for them to be somewhat prepared for the world as I see it." He said he knew I would be safe living in the home we were in, and he believed I was strong enough to go on without him should that day come.

From my perspective, the Lord heard those words and believed the same. He had seen that my husband was tired of the constant struggle. He knew that I willingly spent my life living in my husband's shadow, and I would never achieve my purpose in life living that way. I understand that now, but I only wish I had understood it then and that it didn't take bringing my husband home with him to get me to that realization.

My heart tells me that my husband knew his work was done on earth, he knew he was going home, and that he would not have had it any other way. He was tired of fighting, tired of stressing, and now, he is in paradise and at peace as he watches over us while we fight to reach our destination and fulfill our purpose in this life.

My husband was not perfect, I am not perfect, and our marriage was in no way perfect. We did not always let God lead, but we did believe in our marital vows, we did understand our job as parents, and we knew how we were supposed to live according to his word.

We made mistakes, we failed God more than once, and we followed the devil's lead a time or two along the way. We were not proud of those misguided choices, and I continue to ask God to forgive us for those. The Ten Commandments are the guide the Lord has given us for the life he expects us to live. Most, if not all, are not hard to follow if you carry yourself as a decent human being in this world, but we are all being challenged to see if we are capable of such a task.

The lesson to be learned is that we cannot live a life that lives up to those rules if we don't first believe in our hearts that a greater power than us exists. If we can't feel the punishment that comes from disobeying his word, then we have not humbled ourselves enough to accept him in our lives and have not allowed him to take the lead on our path in life.

I know that I would not have made it through all of the storms throughout my life and I would not be achieving all that I am if I did not believe. If I did not surrender and let him take the reins to guide me on my path in life, I would not be living some of my dreams today.

Looking back through the years I spent with my husband, I can see now that life was quite messy for us. I'm not sure we had any of the right answers for making it through the struggles the way we did. For me, I just gave everything to God. I was tired of fighting and feeling angry and broken all the time. As for my husband, I think he was tired of fighting the world and the demons and afraid of the outcome if he didn't stop giving in. We were both quite aware of how life, living, and fighting were affecting our marriage.

Everyone in this world has a way that they handle their pressures, a way that they work things out or deal with anything that comes their way in life. I refuse to stop caring, I refuse to see the bad, and I choose to only focus on the good. I won't give up; I won't stop trying, and I will never allow any failure to get the best of me. I will not walk away from someone I love, and I will never give up on them or our relationship without exhausting every effort I can. This is how I am made.

I never gave up on him or us. We never stopped loving each other; he just stopped loving life. He was frustrated, as we all are, with the world today. He never handled stress well, and he could never see an end to the struggle or learn to just let the struggle go and let God take over. He could not see that what he had was enough; he wanted more, and wanting more is great but never to the expense that you stop enjoying and appreciating what you already have. It is never okay to lose sight of the blessings right in front of you.

We are blessed with the gift of life—not only ours, but the lives of our children. We are blessed with all of the beauty that surrounds us and the beautiful Earth God has given us; we just have to take the time to see it.

We as humans are charged with making life what we choose it to be. It is each one of us that makes our world what it is. We do not need all the material things we desire. The good Lord gave us everything we need to survive on this planet. It is our own weakness, greed, lust, and selfishness that will come to destroy us all if we let it.

When we let ourselves fall on a crutch, such as alcohol, drugs, cigarettes, violence, and gambling, it is then that we destroy ourselves. We let the devil in and choose the easy way out of our life battles, and the reality is, we just make it harder. Using any substance to make us feel better about our lives does not take away the struggles; they will still be there when you come down from the high. I used to tell my husband, "The only thing you are doing is adding to your anguish in life because tomorrow, you will not only still have the same problems, but you will feel like garbage, hold remorse, and have an angry wife to add to your troubles."

You see, you will not take away your troubles with these crutches but instead add to them. Some of these crutches cause diseases such as cancer, cirrhosis of the liver, and heart failure. Other crutches can lead to financial destruction, death by accident or overuse, a lifetime in jail, loss of family, and so on. We are not finding solutions in these evils but merely Band-Aids to lessen the pain and cover up the wounds.

The point is we may not always create the problems we have, but we certainly find ways to make them worse and dig ourselves greater holes that we must dig our way out of. Sometimes, we dig those holes so deep that we can't find our way out, and then it becomes too late.

Our beautiful life is gone. What I would like to share with you is that five months after I lost my husband, I was driving home from running an errand with regard to my husband's death. I was sobbing uncontrollably, and as I turned a corner in town, a truck pulled in front of me. The entire back end of the truck had the Bible verse John 3:16 written across it, and at that very moment, I realized that God was telling me my husband's life was not over but everlasting, and that he would always be with me.

I decided right then to not begin digging my own holes and to let go and let God. He has not failed me yet.

They call it grieving when you are filled with heartache after losing someone. I am not a fan of that term. I call it missing the presence of someone, holding on to a never ending love, learning how to keep on living, and fighting to find the positive in it all. I do not think my so-called grieving will ever really end because I will never stop loving my husband or missing his presence, and I will never stop fighting to keep on.

I do not believe we are ever supposed to lose our love for those that meant so much to us because that love helps us to continue on. That life we shared with them gave us the baseline that guides our lives. It taught us how to do things differently if given a next time around and gives us the strength to keep going. Their presence will never go away; it is always with you because they never stop loving you either.

I believe God is challenging us to find our happiness and our purpose and to live our greatest life possible. We must have faith that he will be our strength and our guide in achieving it all.

Chapter 6

Every moment in our lives is a given. It is how we choose to live in those moments that determines our happiness. We need to live with gratitude in our hearts for every moment we are given, and when we begin to live a life of constant gratitude for every aspect of our lives and our allowance to live, then and only then will we truly find our greatest happiness.

If you read my last book, you may remember when I asked, "When does life start to be about my happiness?" The answer to that question is that it always was about my happiness—I just didn't see it. My happiness was in my children's smiles, my husband's pride in me, and in knowing that I was doing my best at being a mother, a wife, a daughter, and as a person altogether. The part I was missing was achieving the things I really wanted in life, living life the way I wanted to and not how my husband thought was best. To me, at the time, I was okay following his lead and living life the way we were. I was willing to let go of the things I wanted to achieve; my family meant more to me than my desires did and more to me than I did to myself.

If you have not found that one thing in life that makes you undeniably the happiest you have ever felt in your life; if you haven't taken the time to slow down, regroup, and refocus; and if you haven't allowed yourself the chance to reach out and take your life back to make it yours and to have everything in this lifetime that makes you your absolute happiest, then you are wasting the precious life that God gave you, and life is way too short to keep wasting it. Stop what you are doing right now, and think about what makes you the happiest you have ever been or what could make you the happiest you could ever be, and go after it!

Make today your new beginning. I know it sounds unreasonable and screams unrealistic. I know we have to pay our bills and make a living. I know it is a scary thought, and it feels ridiculous and stupid to even imagine just walking away from what we are doing now and walking toward what we have always wanted out of life instead, but it is possible. It is realistic, reasonable, ridiculous, and stupid, but you can do it. I know this because I am doing it today.

There is nothing unrealistic about wanting to live your life to the fullest and throwing all the cards in to do whatever it takes to make your dreams a reality.

It is unreasonable to think that we must live miserably our whole lives just to pay our bills, eat, and keep on because the reason for living should never be defined by the necessities. We need to stay alive, but by the way we choose to live and by the way we feel about the life we are living. We should be considering why we were put on this earth and what our purpose is supposed to be while we are living on it.

God did not put us on this earth just to maintain life. He had a purpose for us. We are supposed to ensure that the lives we live have purpose, and that we are responsible for our own fulfillment in life and our own happiness. Not just the momentary happiness in a day, but the everyday, all-day happiness that we desire to have. Despite all the jokes and sarcasm, it does not come in a bottle or a pill, a cancer stick, a powder, a needle, or any other form of delusional happiness. It comes from within you and through him.

It is ridiculous to believe that you can never have the happiness you want in life because you cannot afford it or to think it is not in your reach financially or there is not enough time in life left to achieve it. This is simply not true; it is all within your reach and achievable. If you honestly believe and you trust in yourself and in the Lord, you can achieve anything. You can afford more than you think, you can reach for it, and you can make life everything you want it to be.

It is stupid if you believe anything less than that. If you continue to work that miserable job that you hate and stay stagnant in a life you despise just to make a living and live day by day, get up, go to work, come home, and go to bed. No one wants to live that life, and no one has to. The only thing stupid about stopping what you are doing and taking your life back, no matter the cost, is that you have not done it yet!

There is still time, so stop what you are doing, look at the life you are currently living, ask yourself if you are genuinely happy, step outside, smell the air, listen to the birds, and feel the breeze in your hair. Take a leap of faith, ask God to stand beside you, and see you through and find your true happiness.

Money is not what makes us happy, and if it is, it should not be. You are missing the true and only real meaning of life. What money buys us provides us momentary happiness, not a lifetime of it.

I am not sharing this to steer you into a falsehood. I am sharing this because I have done it. Trust me, it is possible, it is realistic, it is reasonable, and it is the best feeling ever! I hope you find it.

After years of struggling, fighting, and feeling quite often broken, I started to believe that was just the way life was supposed to be. When my husband passed away, it was just another bullet in an already open wound, and I figured that it was a wound that was never meant to heal. I believed that this was just the life I was meant to live, that I was meant to always battle and live in strife. Until I told myself not anymore.

One of my sons had asked me to make a list of places I wanted to see in this world and vacations I would like to take, and as I was writing them down, I realized I still have an entire lifetime to live, God willing, and I decided that I am going to live it.

It suddenly became a reality to me that there was no one to discuss ideas with or to question my choices—there was only me. If I were going to be happy in my life, I had to make the choices that would bring me my greatest happiness, and I have started doing just that.

My first step was to give everything to God. To have faith that whatever he chooses for me in this remainder of my life, he will never let me fall, and it will be those things that give me the greatest fulfillment in my life. I could not have made a wiser decision.

Yes, I am doing the footwork, writing my book, getting it published, falling in love again, taking care of my youngest son, moving to a house on a lake, and paying the financial cost to do so, but the Lord is seeing me through it all.

The choices he is making for me, I could not have chosen better myself. One of those choices was to change direction of what I do for a living. No, I will never give up on my license as a nurse, but I am choosing to make this nursing career work for me instead of me working for it and being unhappy, unappreciated, and feeling little to no reward for what I do.

Since I was a little girl, I always wanted to be a nurse or a doctor. It wasn't until I worked in this field that I realized today's nurse or doctor is not the same as they were when I was younger. The world has changed those titles, and now, a registered nurse is treated like a grunt worker, no better than a day laborer, and the doctors no longer have a voice to practice the way they think is best or the time to be personable and really care. It truly breaks my heart.

It was not until I started working as a one-on-one nurse for a special needs child through a school system where I lived that I truly saw the reward of being a nurse today. Oddly enough, falling in love again and choosing to live with him on the lake found me making the choice to leave that perfect job for me, but that job helped me see what I genuinely wanted out of my career and what I desire to do. I will never settle for less than that again.

Life has dumped many less-than-desirable piles of hurt on me. Losing my husband was among the greatest of those hurts. I am not now, nor will I ever be, indestructible, but with my faith in God, I am capable of achieving all my dreams and living a life that makes me as happy as I choose to be.

Life gives us all hands we are never ready to be dealt, but it is the reaction we have to the cards we acquire that decides whether we win the game.

My youngest son is a shining example of that. Between my late husband and I, we have pulled him through four school districts, and every time, this boy chose to adjust like a champion to each and every one. He is my inspiration every day. He is an amazing soul, and I am very proud of him. He reminds me to always let my spirit shine. You get one life, live it to the fullest. He is my spirit.

I am, of course, proud of all my boys the way they handle their own life battles and the success they are achieving, but my youngest proves the theory that if you handle what is thrown at you with positivity and you choose to never accept defeat, you will always win.

Each one of my children inspires me. My third oldest has a heart of gold, with the greatest sense of direction. He is my comfort and my rock. He reminds me that money does not buy happiness; it is merely a tool to achieve your own desires in life. He is my sense of direction and my mental strength.

My second oldest has the greatest confidence, and he is a true leader. He has taught me to always want more out of life and to never stop reaching for my dreams; he is my passion, my toughest critic, and my inspiration to be confident in myself and my choices in life. He is my soul.

My oldest is my strength. He is my sunshine and my inspiration to never stop fighting. He teaches me that you are only as strong as you choose to be and how important you are to your own self. He reminds me to be healthy and to care for the entirety of myself, not just my mind and soul, but my entire body and the care it needs to live a long and happy life. He is my heart.

My boys are the reason that I continue to fight and persevere through every storm. They are the light in my life, and they give me hope and the desire to always be their inspiration as well. They are my greatest achievement and four of the biggest reasons for my smile today. They are my everything.

There is a song out there that says, "O Lord, I'd be lost but for the grace of God," and I cannot think of anything truer in my life than that.

Every one of my blessings in life have been given to me through God's grace. Every step I continue to take and every hurdle I have climbed have all been possible because of God's love for me and the strength I carry through Him.

So the truthful answer to that initial question, When does life start to be about my happiness?, is when you seek your happiness through how happy you make God with you and your life choices. This is when your every happiness in life becomes real and true. This is when your soul finds eternal peace, and everything in your life suddenly feels perfect. This is when you feel undeniably blessed by God.

> *But by the grace of God I am what I am: and his grace which was bestowed upon me was not in vain; but I laboured more abundantly than they all: yet not I, but the grace of God which was with me.*
> (1 Corinthians 15:10–12)

Chapter 7

Why is it that human beings are always reaching for more? Why are we never content with what we already have? Why does it seem like being healthy, having four walls around us, a roof over our head, and food to eat never feels like enough? Why do some believe that there is not a God? Because if there was, we would not be suffering or enduring diseases. Perhaps we are just greedy people that will never find fulfillment because we are too busy wanting more.

God has blessed me with everything I was aspiring to have, but none of it came easy. I have spent my entire life fighting for every happy moment, every material desire, and every bit of peace I could get. I have spent thirty-two years paying bills, raising a family, working alongside, and fighting with my spouse to get to where I am today. I have endured emergency surgeries, difficult pregnancies, watching a child suffer from diseases, and losing my spouse.

I look at my life today and I have my health, four amazing children, a beautiful home, a wonderful man, and his two beautiful children in my life, and I live on the water like I always wanted to, yet I am still struggling to feel completely fulfilled. I have never been happier with my life, and still, I feel sadness and burden.

I don't blame God because I know the world and myself cause my pain. I live with the burden of never having enough money, the heartache of never understanding why someone I love left me so soon, and watching the faces of my children as they feel the hurt and anguish of missing their father. The frustration of not being able to help my mother find her happiness in life and watching my family members struggle and suffer without being able to fix it all the way my heart wants to.

None of these things came about because God said "take that" or because he did not do anything to prevent it from happening in the first place. All these things occurred because every one of us made choices in our lives that led us to these moments and into these situations. My husband lived the life he wanted to, and his habits and inability to handle stress weakened his heart and caused his early death. Should my children and I suffer for that? No, but we do because of his choices, not God's.

My mother is like most of us—financially burdened because of the choices we made. We overspent, and we embellished on our wants in life and made it harder to take care of our own needs. We are not lacking money because God isn't flourishing us with lottery winnings or leading us to gold mines. We do these things to ourselves and along with the government's hand in our pockets because of our own greed as a society.

My family's health suffers because they don't take care of themselves. They choose to have bad habits all their lives, and their bodies are paying the price for it now. Diseases are not manifested by God; they are brought on by the chemicals and the environment we have created on this earth. God makes the choice to take us out of our suffering and bring us home to paradise with him.

We are provided the freedom to make our own choices in this life, and it is the choices we make that decide how we live and die. God helps those who help themselves, and we as a people are not very good at doing the right things to help ourselves from suffering. Even my son's diseases were not brought on by God but were instead brought on, I believed, by me. I have to believe that the way I took care of myself and my unborn child during my pregnancy may have led to his suffering, and for that, I will always be sorry.

It's not that we intentionally set out to hurt ourselves, but instead, I believe it is that we have not allowed ourselves to have faith in God that he would see us through the storms, and we have not made the decision to live through God and be happy with what we already have. We have taken advantage of the gifts God has provided us from the beginning—gifts like the plant life surrounding us that provides us oxygen and the ability to breathe; the fruits and vegetables, oats and grains that keep us healthy and our bodies strong; the water that flows around us that washes our bodies and feeds the plant life that keep our bodies alive; the animals that walk and live among this earth that provide us with substance and nutrients for our bodies to survive; the warmth of the sun that feeds our soul and strengthens our bodies; the light of the moon to guide us when it's dark and see us through the night.

God gave us life and the Earth we live on. We can make it a joyous life or a life full of strain and torture. It is up to us how we choose to live while we have a life on this beautiful planet to live.

Sometimes, it's not so easy to see through the frustrations and the anger over what we haven't accomplished or what we are struggling to achieve. We have a hard time seeing past what we want and don't have, and it's always easier to blame someone or something else for our downfalls and our weaknesses. Most of us do just that.

No one ever wants to look in the mirror and reprimand the person looking back at them. It is not easy to take the fault and accept the blame, and for some, when they do, they can't live with it. You don't have to hold onto it; you just need to realize it and do better.

You need to let go of the strife going on in your mind and your heart and let God take over as the leader on your path in this life. Let him show you how happy you can really be. You will still struggle from time to time, but you will learn to handle it better, and you will find peace in knowing that you are no longer enduring the struggles alone. You will find the acceptance that God will never let you fall if you just believe.

We don't survive on this earth because of what the government affords us or the employer pays us. We survive on this earth through the choices we make and by the grace of God.

It's not up to us to decide our path in life, but it is up to each one of us to determine how our path will end. We determine what kind of legacy we will leave behind and what imprint we will have made on this earth during our lifetime.

Will it be one of positivity? Will you have been a beacon of light or one of darkness and despair? Will your children and their children and the children after them find a beaten path of arduous work and endurance that leaves them a brightly lit path to be proud of and to follow? Or will it be a dimly lit, unkept path of destruction and demise—one with no hope or promise for what lies ahead of them?

I never took the time to ponder on any of this earlier in my life, but suddenly, after losing my husband all too soon, I realize how short life truly is and how valuable we are as human beings to the loved ones we leave behind. In truth, I see now how much each one of us has an impact on all those we touch throughout our path in life. So for me, I choose to make every effort to be an inspiration, a beacon of light, and a positive force that leaves my children, my loved ones, and all of those I have touched in this life, smiling, feeling loved, appreciated, and cared for.

I choose to leave a brightly lit path behind me that opens the way for others to follow and for them to feel at peace with themselves, knowing that their job was done well.

Fall is here. The entire scene of the autumn colors on the leaves, the crisp air all around, and the rushing of the waters from the cool breeze is, without a doubt, the most spectacular canvas designed by God.

As I sit looking at the crisp fallen leaves on my deck and the grass below, I am reminded of a song that was so dear to my late husband—a song his mother used to sing to him when he was a child—"Come Little Leaves." This song was a precious memory to him, one he held dear to his heart. He not only wrote down all the words, which I still have, but he sang this song to each one of our boys when they were younger.

There are moments throughout my life now when a memory of him is triggered by a sound, a song, a view, a scent, and even sometimes just certain actions throughout my day. Sometimes, they are unpleasant memories, but mostly, they are genuinely sweet memories of him and the beautiful mind and heart he held. He truly was an old soul, and he always found beauty and specialness in the most precious things.

He believed in tradition and keepsakes and being delicate with the things that hold unmeasurable value. Things like songs, poems, trinkets from ancestors, and memories from the past.

He looked at the beauty in nature that surrounds us, and he always held the greatest love and appreciation for it all. It destroyed him to think that we as humans were taking advantage of what we had and slowly working to tear it all down and abolish all our freedoms that allow us the ability to live among this beauty as we see fit and enjoy it all without any inhibition.

To this day, his memory reminds me to always see the beauty that this earth holds and to take in and appreciate every bit of it every moment that I can. He reminds me to not only hear the song but to listen to its every word and feel it within me. He reminds me to appreciate the things I own and the value they hold and to take care of what you have.

He reminds me that your home should be your happiness, your place of peace and serenity, one of tranquility and a feeling of contentment. Take pride in your home and in yourself, and live passionately and with a humbleness that continues to remind you to look around you and take in what so greatly surrounds you.

The best thing about it is that the most beautiful treasures that surround you are free; you don't have to work to enjoy them, but you do have to take the initiative to stop and see it, take it in, and learn to appreciate its value.

"Come Little Leaves"—it's just a song, but to him, it was one of the little things that meant the entire world to him. It was always nestled deep in his heart and in his memories that he held so dear, and every fall, he was reminded of its words and his mother's gentle voice sharing it with him.

We are often so busy in this life that we lose ourselves and our memories, and those moments in our lives that we are supposed to take in and treasure are quickly gone and long forgotten. We get one life, folks. Step away from the job, step away from the electronic devices, and step into your treasure box. Step outside, and take in your free gifts from God. Stop and listen to the words in the song, feel the artist's thoughts, and endure your own feelings from the words and the melody. Think about some of your greatest memories and moments in this life.

Be alive, not just living. The leaves may have fallen, but they are a constant reminder that no matter how many times we fall, we can fall with grace, regenerate, and find new life. The colors in the leaves are a sign of age and change before death reaches the door. As we get older, we must remember to live our lives with beauty, dignity, and grace so that our last fall leaves a beautiful memory for the ones we love.

Perhaps it's not a question of whether we feel completely fulfilled in life but, instead, whether we have touched others' lives with the light they needed to help them feel complete and a sense of fulfillment in their life.

Just maybe, the sadness and burden we feel in our lives is meant to be there to remind us to stay humble and be appreciative of the lives we have been given.

My husband's mother will always be that inspiration to me—one that reminds me that taking the extra step, creating from scratch, and putting your love into everything you do lay a foundation of comfort and sweetness toward everyone you share it with, and she continues to bestow her special care for the treasures of the past, the beauty of today, and the promise of tomorrow to my children and myself. I can never thank her enough for sharing her son with me and being that extra guide in becoming a better mother to my own children.

As a mother, I know that I would endure everything thrown at me in this world to make sure that my children never have to. There are many treasures in this world that I hold dear to me, but the greatest of those are my children, and I choose to clear every land mine and take every questionable path so that they may live their greatest life, knowing mom lit the way for them.

As a widow, I know that my job is now twofold, and I must play the roles of both mom and dad, but with this, I know that even though he is not present in this life, my husband will always be present in their minds and hearts and will continue to guide them throughout their lives.

It's funny, we are coming up on two years since my husband passed, and I thought when the day of his passing came up this year, I would be okay. But I could not know that my internal soul would feel differently and assume control over me, bringing me to uncontrollable tears out of nowhere and reminding me that there will always be a piece of me missing and that the anguish of losing him that fateful day will never go away.

Yes, this time of year will always bring that painful memory in to play, not because I am supposed to suffer, but because losses like this leave a permanent scar on your heart and in your memory. These embedded memories serve as a reminder that life is unpredictable, and death even more so. They are meant to humble us and to help us see that the life we live and the way it ends or when it ends is not entirely up to us, but what is up to us is how we choose to live the life we have while we have it.

We can choose to live a life filled with happiness, or we can choose to live in complete misery—that choice is ours. It is the choices we make that control our destiny in life, and I have faith in the Lord to decide for me, whether the direction I am headed in is the right path for me, and I know he will never steer me wrong.

We are not given a magic wand to make all our wishes come true or a crystal ball to see into our future and guide us toward our next move on this journey. What we are given is a strong mind to give us perception and a heart to feel what is right and wrong. Some of us follow a gut instinct with regard to the right and wrong choices. We are all given the opportunity to find our faith in the Lord and let him guide us toward the life we are meant to live.

I can never go back and prevent my husband's destination with death or change the choices we made and take away the struggles we went through, but I can learn from the life we lived and what may have led to his death so soon. I can use those lessons to change my own direction in life and make better choices for myself and my children from this day forward.

Like the leaves in every autumn that go out with such beauty and fall with such unsurmountable grace, I will choose to see my husband's passing as a beautiful reminder to live my life so that one day, I might fall with the same amazing and beautiful grace.

Chapter 8

It is not enough to hope that we live a life full of peace and happiness. We all want to leave a positive lasting impression on the ones we love and the ones we have connected with throughout our lives. We all want to believe that when our time comes, we will have left this earth with some sort of dignity and grace. Who wouldn't want to pass on knowing we have done our job here on earth well, but who really gets the opportunity to contemplate that before their life here is over?

The best way to know what kind of life you lived and what kind of impression you made is to live your life well right now. Be happy with the life you are living because when you are, that happiness within you will shine on everyone around you.

There is already so much in this world to get us down and make us feel as if life is miserable and unfair. So why be someone who adds to that? Why not be the light in an already dark and sinister world? Why not see the beauty in this world rather than the evil and the corrupt? We know that exists; we do not need to give it a spotlight.

People like my husband did not know how to see past it. That's not to say he wasn't a happy-go-lucky guy. It is just to help you understand that he was great at letting others see his happy, but behind the scenes, the stress he was enduring from the world around him ate him up, and he let it. He let the world play him like a fiddle, and I was letting him and the world do it to me too.

I suffer from mental abuse that has occurred, probably all my life, in some form or another, and from many different sources along the way, but don't we all suffer from some sort of mental anguish in our lives? Some sort of hurt that hit us at the very core of our soul? I venture to guess that each and every one of us has not only endured some form of hurt toward ourselves but has doled some out as well. Does that make it okay? Of course not.

The reality I am coming to terms with now is that I only suffer from this abuse because I accepted it as truth, and I allowed it to hurt me. The interesting thing is that once this form of hurt is embedded into you, you are always living in a world of caution, of reflex, and in constant defense mode. It just becomes a part of who you are.

The even greater reality is that you do not see how it has profoundly affected you, and the people doing it do not even realize what they are doing. They are reflecting their guilt onto you for their actions and making you feel as if you are to blame for their behaviors. They push you into a state of vulnerability, they take advantage of your kindness and your willingness to tolerate their attacks, and they keep you in that state of belief because you let them. You have lost the confidence in yourself and the ability to fight back. You eventually learn to give up, and you accept the pain.

The greatest reality is what I am realizing today. This happens to you and beats you down emotionally and mentally *because you let it*! It's not enough to be kind and loving, generous, and caring. You have to be strong, independent, confident, and somewhat callous, but most of all, you have to know your worth and believe in yourself.

It doesn't matter what anyone else believes; you believe in you, and God believes in you.

Never let anyone make you feel less, and never let anyone control the narrative or place the guilt they hold onto you. Never place yourself in a position of such vulnerability that they feel power over you. No loud voice or intense temper, form of guilt, or greater physical strength should ever be enough to make you submissive to their abuse. What you must understand is they are not powerful—they are weak. So weak that they can't even accept their own guilt and their own wrongdoings, and they refuse to take the blame for their own actions.

It is not easy to swallow your pride and take responsibility for your actions.

Know who you are, believe in yourself, be in control of your life, and have faith in yourself and in God that your strength is awesome, your worth is immeasurable, and you are an incredible human being that deserves the best.

No one is perfect, and no one deserves to carry themselves as such other than God himself.

The hard part of this other than the pain you endure is that it sometimes comes from people you love, and for some of us, you don't stop loving them because of it; you just stop loving you. I have always been someone who chooses to see the better in someone and not one to attack back, but to offer greater love and love them no less because I know the best part of who they are and what causes them to be this hurtful person is not who I believe they really are. This does not make it okay, but for me, it made it a little easier to endure. Of course, I had no idea how it was truly affecting me.

What I do know is that I choose to let the hurt go and only remember the wonderful moments, the best of who they are and of who we are together, and that does not make me a foolish person. It makes me the better person.

Everyone has issues, and every one of us makes mistakes, and we all live with imperfections and pain that sometimes cause unintentional feelings or behaviors toward the ones we love. But it's the intentional actions that we hurl at each other for our own self-gain that are unacceptable and damaging to the ones we love. We live in a world of dog-eat-dog, and it is unfortunate and sad.

We as a society may never change these behaviors, but we as individuals can start by carrying ourselves with dignity and pride. We can choose to be better than that. We can raise our own children to carry themselves with better moral character, to be respectful yet intolerant to other people's garbage, and to stand up for themselves while at the same time, standing for others as well. No one should feel the need to belittle or judge another.

For those who have endured such abuse, it takes time to heal, and you will heal. Do not let these actions harden you. Just know that you will never allow them again, and you never deserve them. For those who love someone healing from such pain, give them time, be understanding, and for goodness' sake, don't add to their hurt.

This is not for you to fix—it is for you to stand by them and love them, comfort them, and encourage them.

Let your loved ones find their strength the way they need to, not the way you think they should. Just understand whatever it is they need to make them feel confident in themselves, and don't take that as an offensive action toward you.

They are not trying to separate themselves from you but from their old self. They are learning to be strong and proud, resilient, and independently powerful in order to heal what has been broken for so long.

It is not a separation from you, but a reunification with themselves and the person they believe themselves to be and want to be. We can all use a rebuild from time to time and a reconnection to our inner self, our true character, and our moral sanctity within ourselves.

I know I am working on just that. It's been a long time since I worked on who I am, and I am excited to find out. One thing I know for sure is I am someone who deserves to be treated with dignity, respect, and love, and I believe in myself. I know I can do all things through Christ because he strengthens me.

So here is a thought: be proud of who you are, be humble and be kind, be patient and understanding with the ones you love, and have faith and believe in yourself and always know that when it seems as if no one cares, God is always there.

It was not until after my husband passed that I decided to stop watching political news or any regular TV anymore. I stopped watching TV at all for that matter. I decided that I would no longer let anyone else decide how I would feel or impress on me any negative connotations, period.

I stopped caring what the commentators were saying, and I realized that none of them were in this business to make my life better. None of them were looking out for me, and not a single one was really being truthful about anything.

I know this: I get one life, and I have only one choice while I am living it to live it! So I am going to live it well. I am going to enjoy my life by appreciating the beauty that this earth has to offer me and not letting the garbage on TV and the political rhetoric being spewed destroy how I feel about the world I live in. I will choose for myself how the world around me looks and how I feel about it. I will choose the kind of life I am going to live, and no political decisions can ruin that unless I let them.

I will not let anyone or anything take away my happiness. I am the only one in charge of the choices for my life, and there is only one who can take exception with those choices, and that is the Lord.

I have held a lot of anger toward my husband for letting the world get the best of him. I felt as if he was only thinking of his own self and what he suffered with. He never stopped to think of the pain he would be causing us with his actions. I also feel a great deal of heartache for him that he suffered with so many demons and felt so let down by life.

Just as we learn to have faith in the Lord, we must learn to have faith in others, and that is not always easy. I am guessing most of us have put our faith in someone or something at one time or another and counted on them or it to be reliable for us, and that faith didn't always pan out, but that doesn't mean we should give up or feel as if our whole world is over. We should not assume that there is no hope or place blame on those that did not come through for us. It just means that we need to move on, we need to keep trying, and we must continue to have faith that life will work out and God will see us through.

At the end of the day, the reality is the world is not hurting us—we are hurting ourselves. We are allowing ourselves to lose hope, to feel let down, and to be affected by someone's actions or lack thereof. What we should be doing is believing in ourselves and never allowing anyone or anything to get the best of us. It is when we start losing our faith in humanity and in ourselves that we begin to lose our faith in God, and it is then that we lose our opportunity to understand his purpose for our lives on this earth.

The magic and beauty of life is that when we do find our purpose, that is when we truly start to live.

I know I am finding mine. Have you found yours?

Chapter 9

I know losing someone valuable in your life—someone who means everything to you and someone you spent a great deal of your life with—is hard. I know learning to get on with your life and to let go of the pain in your heart is difficult. I know the concept of moving on and starting over seems crazy and even sometimes feels as if we are forgetting them or making them see that we have stopped caring, but it's simply not true. In fact, I believe that they want us to enjoy our lives and to keep living for them, and they would never want us to be miserable, angry, and suffering emotionally for the rest of our lives.

When I lost my husband, I almost lost myself too. I didn't feel life would be worth living without him in it. What I was not able to see then that I can see now is that he is always in this life with me, always. He left this earth, but he will always be with the ones he loved and the ones who loved him. His spirit and his memory will never die. He knows that everyone has a path to follow, and we are still making our way along ours. I spent thirty-two years with this man; he is everything I know about life up to this point. I will never stop remembering the positives he shined into my life, but I know that I need to move on, and I need to live my life my way. The man I am with today, he and I will never live the same way that my late husband and I did. We must start our own journey together and create our own way of life as a couple, and that is a good thing.

Every one of us has been through challenges in our lives. Every one of us has felt pain and endured sorrow. It is how we handle it that makes us who we are and decides how our life will continue on. It is all riding on how much faith we have in ourselves and in God. Without faith in our lives, we have no ability or desire to push ourselves to live the best life possible. We must trust and have faith that there is a higher power that will always want the best for us and will never steer us wrong.

There will always be difficulties in life, but they are only meant to make us stronger and to help us learn to change direction toward a better path.

Some of the things I struggle with the most are to stop living in the past and to stop running my life concerned about how my husband would feel or what he would think about the things I am doing or the way I am living. He is gone, and I must go on.

Finding your purpose in life is an ongoing challenge. Learning how your life is supposed to be or what is planned for you is guided by faith. You are merely the pebble in the sand, and God is the creator that picks you up, dusts you off, molds you into his perception of who you are meant to be, and then allows you to find the polish that makes you shine. It is when he sees the promise in you that his light provides you with the greatest glow.

I will always miss my husband, and I will always love him, but losing him has shown me that life is too short to not live it giving it everything you've got. His being in my life was part of life's plan that God has for me. My purpose in life was not meant to dissolve upon his passing but to continue on. I was meant to find love more than once, and I believe I was always supposed to find both of the men in my life. They each have a specific purpose in my life.

My late husband helped me to grow and find strength and confidence in myself, and he gave me my greatest gifts in life—my four beautiful children. My love now will help me to reach for the stars and achieve my greatest potential in this world. He will help me to keep believing in myself because he believes in me so greatly.

I believe my purpose in life is to share my story with all of you. To share my challenges and my beliefs with hopes of inspiring or helping someone else along the way. My purpose in life is to be the best me I can be. I hold no wand; I carry no crown on my head, and I have no unlimited wealth to spread around. I only have my heart and my words to share, but I believe what I have to share is worth sharing, and above all else, that the work I am doing now is my true purpose in this life.

There are life coaches, books, videos, and more that can guide you on how to run your life, to find prosperity, and to live with purpose, but only you can make any of those things happen, and it is always your choices in life that lead you to your destinations in this world. When I was a child, I aspired to be a teacher one day. Then as I started to grow and become acquainted with others in my life, I had dreams to be a nurse or a doctor. In some way, I wanted to help make a difference in others' lives.

I accomplished that dream of being a nurse, and I was overjoyed at my achievement. I worked hard to get there, and I acquired two degrees in my path to what I thought was the right destination for me. During my quest to achieve my second degree, I lost my husband of twenty-seven years. It was then I realized that being a nurse was not my destination in life, and it was never my full purpose—it was merely an achievement I needed to fulfill along the way. Being a nurse takes a special person for sure. It just wasn't the reality I believed it to be for me.

I worked hard, and I spent a great deal of money and time away from my family to get to that degree and to reach that determined level in my life. I still believe it is a wonderful choice to make, and I am proud of my earned titles in life—wife, mother, registered nurse, and most recently, author. Of those titles, my most treasured are being a mother and an author—the two professions that truly speak of who I am as a person, the two that hold the most value and make me feel the most rewarded in my entire life. I know that they are two destinations on my path in life that the Lord has everything to do with and where my path has shined the brightest thus far.

Your purpose in life Is not presented to you like a game board, but it is certainly very similar to the game of life. We are offered choices, we are taxed, we are given the opportunity to change direction at many given points, and someday, if we make just enough right choices along the way, we will find our every happiness after all the struggles. It is then that we can say we had a great life, and when

God is ready to take us home, we will be ready. We will know that we did our best and left behind a shining light for others to follow.

Finding your purpose takes time and effort. It is something that you will be continuing to do for most of your life.

Have you ever found something in your life that you are really good at? Something that makes you feel an incredible sense of joy every time you do it? Have you ever said to yourself, Man I wish I could do that for a living. What an awesome job that would be? Have you ever heard the words, "If you believe it, you can achieve it"?

I always thought that part of living was to work your whole life so that you could have something to live for, but the truth is you should be living your whole life so that you never have to feel like you are working a day in it.

After watching my husband work every day for twenty-eight years as mechanic and hate almost every minute of it, I concluded that his working was only paying the bills. It wasn't fulfilling any satisfaction in his life. In fact, it was making all of us miserable because he was miserable. I'm sorry that his life was served that way, but only he could have changed it, and his choices were what led him there. They were not the right choices for him or the real destination he was supposed to arrive to. He made wrong decisions that directed him down the wrong path—certainly not the path God intended for him.

Somewhere along the way, he did well in life because the good Lord took him home to paradise. I know this because I believe in the Lord, and my heart tells me so.

After seeing my husband suffer in misery, I know now that I must make better choices, and I have decided to live my best life by living the way that makes me the happiest. I will never let a job be my life. I was taught a while back that JOB stands for *just over broke*. To me, broke doesn't just refer to money but to the way you feel, mentally and physically, in life. No job is worth losing your own self-worth. The ones who love you never want you to feel miserable about the life you are living.

So when you lose someone important to you, someone who meant the world to you, do yourself a favor. Step back and look at the life they led and ask yourself, Were they truly happy? Did they live a life they absolutely loved, or did they work themselves to the bone and miss out on many of the joys they could have been a part of in their lives? Then take a page from their book, and learn what not to do and how to live better before it's too late. Find what your true purpose in life really is, and make it happen.

I am taking lessons from the life my late husband and I lived, and I am choosing to change my direction in life. Living a life of reservation and procrastination is not acceptable; life is just too short for that. I am going to enjoy my life and do all the things that make me happy. I may not find an abundance of wealth in what I do now, but my life will be filled with happiness, love, and a sense of satisfaction, knowing that I served my greatest purpose in this life doing what I truly love.

Writing is a great passion of mine. I don't know if I will ever be a renowned author making great money from my work, but I will be a proud author. I will keep writing books and blogs, and maybe someday, I'll even get the chance to speak on my writings. I intend to start my own business that will include my personal view of the greatest gifts we have been given, my writings, and what inspires me in hopes of inspiring others along the way. All these things will come from my heart and my vision, and I know they will bring me great happiness and pride for the rest of my life.

It's the things we can't hold and the things we can't buy or ever truly own that are the most precious and valuable gifts life has to offer. It's the beauty that surrounds us every day, the new and precious lives we bring into the world, the love we give to one another, the freedom to achieve whatever we desire, and the faith in a higher power that tells us that life is everlasting, and we shall never perish if we just believe.

Life's purpose is not a job—it's a vision, a persistent feeling in the pit of your stomach and deep within your heart that says this is the right path for you. This is where your greatest happiness lives.

As a little girl, I was always proud of my daddy and how hard he worked. I knew that he went to his job every day and worked the extra time every week so that he could give us everything we wanted in life. I loved him for it then, and I love him for it today. What he taught me was to always give your all and to take care of the important things first so that you can enjoy the rewards later. He taught me to be responsible with money and to appreciate what you worked for. He wasn't perfect. He made mistakes, but he gave me a terrific childhood and a world full of love.

My dad had a purpose in his life. He loved the job that he did, and he loved being my dad. He was another part of the path God had paved for my life. He was not my biological father. He came into my life when I was six months old, and he adopted me, but I would never have been the wiser if someone later in my life had not shared this with me. It didn't matter to me then, and it does not matter to me now; to me, he will always be my dad.

As I said, I found out later in life that I had another father out in the world. I met him when I was seventeen. He shared some similarities with my dad—makes sense—which was why my mom fell in love with each one of them at some point in her life. It took me some time to warm up to my biological father, but it has been over thirty years, and he is a very important part of my life now. One man taught me responsibility, and the other helped me to see my worth in the world. Each of them has more than just their own purpose in life, but they also have a purpose in mine. They are part of my path in life. Neither of them is perfect. They have made some poor choices, but both of them have helped me to make better choices in my life, and I love them very much for it.

You see, your purpose in life serves many different aspects of your life. The plan God has for you goes in many directions. You are designed by many different avenues along your path in life. Each one is a step toward your purpose, but it is what you want for yourself and what makes your life feel completely full that leads you to your reason for being. It is what makes everything in your life seem worth it and makes you feel as if your life is everything you wanted it to be. If you are not smiling every day, then you are doing it wrong. You have not found it yet. Don't waste the precious time you have in this life by just accepting where you are.

We all have a dream, and there is a purpose for each and every one of us. It is up to us to decide just how important it is for us to achieve it.

Chapter 10

I learned at a young age how vital the people in my life were to me, and I know now what an important role they have played in who I am today. My parents taught me what real love is. My grandmothers shared their faith with me and guided me in carrying myself like a lady and they will forever continue to be guides in my life with their signs of sky blue pink, daises, and dreams. Through them, school, and a special elementary teacher, I have found my own faith.

In these last few years, I have come to realize that there is something beyond the skies of blue and pink now. Yes, those skies will always be valuable to me. They will always serve a purpose in the direction of my life, but it is my faith in the Lord and in myself that will lead me to my greatest potential in this world.

I can see now that my life does not fit in the box I created for it, and it never should have. I am learning that there is life outside of that box I built, and I need to allow myself to seek it and to fulfill all my dreams. God has provided me the opportunity to find what makes me shine in this world, and I just need to reach out and grab it!

I can keep on living, and all of the signs will still come to guide my way, but this time, I can learn to live for myself and for the Lord. I do not have to give up just because my life has changed. My husband was always terrific at dream building with me and for himself, but he was never exceptionally good at making the dream a reality. He was too easily swayed by the evils in this world that made him feel as if it just wasn't possible. I wish I could have made his dreams come true, and I can't now, but what I can do is make my dreams come true so that he can see that I never gave up, and that all of the dream building that we did together meant something and was worth its weight in gold to me.

It is rather late in my life to believe that I can still accomplish everything I hope to achieve, but I have faith that if I keep fighting toward these dreams and God believes they are part of my destination in the life he has planned for me, then I will succeed.

There is never be a day that goes by that I don't think of my husband or a time that I am not reminded of him by something or someone. He will always be with me wherever I go because he will always own an exceptionally large piece of my heart. We accomplished so much together, we lived a whole lifetime together, and I will always be thankful that he was a part of my life.

I have a better understanding now of the signs my grandmothers send to me, and I will continue to take heed of them as I always have, but I can see that there is a greater reality beyond the colors and their level of hue. There is a never-ending horizon and faith that tells me to look way beyond the blue. A faith that tells me that there is more to life than just what we have been programmed to see. There is an entire world surrounding us that we are missing. A beauty and continuity that goes on around us that, if we take the time to really connect with it, we will quite possibly find the greatest harmony we have ever known in our lives.

I have grown a great deal since my husband's passing, and one certainty I learned very quickly is that I am never alone in this world. I will always have my family, my dearest friends, and the Lord by my side. I know now that all the answers I am searching for do not come from a dollar bill or an item at the store. They are not found on the internet or within any employer's handbook.

Every answer that I need with regard to my life, the prosperity I seek, the peace I pray for, and the choices I make being right for me are given through the Lord and are found in his book and only his book. I know that if I follow the path that he has chosen for me, I will find the greatest love and the greatest joy, and I will live the best life I could have ever dreamed of.

Now, all this being said, I will still make wrong choices because I am human. I will still struggle and feel pain once in a while; it's part of the game of life I spoke of earlier. I will turn left instead of right every now and then, but the Lord will guide me to turn around and go in the right direction because I have faith enough to let him take control of my wheel and lead me to my destination.

I understand if your heart questions my beliefs. I get that you might not be able to see what my soul feels and sees. It is not hard to know that most cannot see past what the world has brainwashed them to see, and I mean that with no disrespect or disregard to anyone reading this because I was there once too. I still have material desires; I still need to pay my bills and take care of my family. I still want all the beautiful things I dream of. The difference is that I know if they are meant to be mine, then I will have them. But if they are not, I will not live a horrible life without them. The difference is that I know now that I don't need to work my life away to be successful in taking care of my family and my home.

I know that my children are much happier when I am happy, when I am not stressed, and when my time is always available to them because I am not swamped with work or exhausted from my day. For me, I found, after losing someone who was invaluable to me, that life is short, and you never know when yours will end. So with the time I have left, I will choose to live mine to the fullest.

I will take what my husband and I understood about the frustrations in life, and I will refuse to ever let them use me again. I will not let them beat me down until I feel like I have nowhere left to turn or there is no hope left. I will tell myself instead, There is nothing in this materialistic world that is worthy enough of taking my happiness from me.

I may never have the financial abilities of a millionaire, but I will live my life as if I am the richest woman in the world. I will take trips if I choose to, I will lay on the beach for a month if I choose to, and I will buy the three-hundred-dollar coat if I want it because at the end of the day, it's my life, and I will live it my way. I will never be controlled by someone else's opinion, calendar, or checkbook, but instead, only by the Lord's will and mine.

Have you ever heard the saying "You are your own worst enemy"? Well, my husband was his, and I was mine. We were working our tails off to achieve all our greatest desires, but what we were failing to see was that everything we already had in life and everything we had already achieved was worth more than we could ever imagine.

We were too busy beating ourselves up and wearing ourselves out to enjoy what we already had—a beautiful family, a wonderful home, our health, the health of our children, and our love for each other. We were single-handedly destroying our own lives because we were not satisfied with what was right in front of us.

I did try to remind him and myself a few times of what we already had, but he was quick to dismiss me saying, "But don't you want more?" And I was easily swayed into believing that I did. After he passed, I said that I would give all of it back—the clothes, the shoes, the gadgets, the cars, all of it—just to have him back. I realized none of it matter to me more than he did. None of it was worth more to me than what we had, our little family, and our love for each other.

Now, more than ever, among all the things I still desire to have, I want to live my life and to be happy with whatever it is that I already have, whether I get those other things or not. Life is too fragile to dismiss it for items that you can never take with you when yours ends. All the things that my husband prized in his life are still here. They didn't go with him, and now, they will never hold the value to anyone than they held to him.

I can't bring him back, I can't undo what has been done, but I can live my life for both of us now in hopes that we can finish life knowing that we still won.

There may never be a brewery, millions in the bank, a hit song, or a practice that I someday run, but there will always be our children and our love that says we succeeded in a job well done.

I never planned to go on without him, but now that I am, I have found that I am certainly blessed to get a second chance with another wonderful man. I thank the Lord for him every day. It's not easy to start a life with someone new and to learn each other's idiosyncrasies, faults, imperfections, behaviors, and beliefs on how life should be, but I know, together, we will figure it all out because our love is true and the Lord brought us together for a purpose even greater than he and I already believe.

Looking beyond the life I once knew and beyond the world I once remember, I can see that I have lived a whole lifetime letting the idea of what everyone else thought the world I lived in should be. I have never given much thought to what I really wanted my world to look like or how I really wanted to live the life I have been blessed to be given. I imagine it would have been better to find a compromise to both of our narratives. Compromise is always important, and with that comes plenty of communication with some disagreements along the way. What we all must understand is that it is okay to disagree with each other, and we will not always be on the same page or feel the same way. We would all live happier lives if we could learn to disagree without being angry over someone else's feelings or thoughts.

We must allow each other to be free to live our lives our way, to compromise when we can, but to be willing to see the other side to every equation and understanding that even as a couple, we do not own each other, and we will always need our individual space and time in life to just be ourselves in this world, without feeling as if we are angering someone or hurting their feelings. We all need personal time and to be able to live our lives being the happiest we can possibly be as individuals and together as one.

Commitment to someone is a beautiful thing. Choosing a person to share your life with and to be your one and only is special, and the love you hold between the two of you is priceless.

The vital part of a committed relationship is to be faithful, honest, and true to each other. You are that person's best friend, greatest confidant, teammate, and only lover, but you hold no dictatorship over their life, and you should never try to. You should have the utmost respect for one another and feel the most passionate love for each other. There should be no question about who holds your heart and soul.

I think with my husband, I loved him so immensely that I allowed him to always control the narrative in our lives, and that was my mistake. I never afforded myself the right to much of an opinion. I believed my job was to be the sweet doting wife. Oops. I'm not saying I never did what I wanted. I'm merely stating that I never took the freedom he did in being him to be me, but I am going to now.

As I said before, my life is quite possibly half over at this point, and I plan to live it out with great adventure, immense joy, and determined purpose because I have one to live.

So many things change after a significant loss in your life—your way of living, your way of thinking, the way you feel, and your perspective on life itself. It is quite amazing how your whole world seems to take on a whole new identity. You see everything in a different light, and some things don't seem to hold the same importance or value to you.

You change immensely as a person, and parts of you change without your control, but it is up to you who you decide to become and how much of you you lose, change, or make anew. Just never allow your heartache to destroy you completely. Find your focus to home in on, your purpose, your reason for being, and most importantly, your reason to live.

Look beyond what is already there, what you already know, who you are right now, and see what could truly be there. Learn from what you are going through and the life you were living, determine who you will be now, and live your life with a new and brighter purpose. Make sure you live as if every day was your last, and let the people that love you learn what a wonderful life you lived so that they can be inspired when you're gone to live theirs with the greatest purpose and know their reason to go on.

That moment when the blue in the sky touches the shades of pink and they blend as one is a majestic wonder indeed, but it is what goes beyond those beautiful colors that holds the greatest magic if we allow ourselves to have faith and believe.

So when you are sitting there in a daze, staring at the sky above you and trying to understand what has just taken place in your life and wondering how you will ever go on, allow yourself to look past what is right in front of you and to have faith that you are never alone and there is always something more waiting for you beyond the horizon that you see. Do not let your life end without purpose, my dear friends.

About the Author

K. L. Nelson is the author of the recently published autobiography *A Life Spiritually Guided by Faith, Daisies, and Sky Blue Pink* as well as the owner and sole writer of a personal opinion blog called Kristabells-ponders.com, where she has written one hundred and forty-four blogs to date. She is currently working on starting an online business with a line of merchandise that displays inspirational quotes from her writings and personal photos she has taken of visions that have inspired her. She is a woman of Christian faith, a mother of four wonderful children, a registered nurse, and now living her dream as a full-time writer and connoisseur of the beautiful treasures that God has provided us all on this amazing planet of Earth.

Her passion is to inspire others to slow down and see the beauty that surrounds them and to live their lives doing what makes them the happiest they have ever been. After losing the love of her life unexpectedly three years ago, she has come to realize that there is so much life we are all missing because we are living to work instead of learning to live. She is an avid believer in having the faith to let God take the wheel and steer you toward the greatest journeys of your life.